FREE TRADE: FREE REIN FOR TRANSNATIONAL CORPORATIONS

By José Víctor Aguilar and Miguel Cavada Diez

Translated by Kathy Ogle

EPICA
Washington, DC

Free Trade: Free Rein for Transnational Corporations

© 2003 EPICA
Ecumenical Program on Central America and the Caribbean
1470 Irving St. NW
Washington, D.C. 20010
202/332-0292; fax 202/332-1184
epicabooks@epica.org

Material originally published in Spanish as
Libre comercio...libertinaje de las trasnacionales
© Asociación Equipo Maíz, 2002, under ISBN 99923-25-22-4
San Salvador, El Salvador,
publicacionesmaiz@hotmail.com

Authors: Miguel Cavada Diez and José Victor Aguilar

Editors: Roberto Quinteros, Marvin Hernández

Translator: Kathy Ogle

English Version Editor: Rebecca Brune

Cover Art: *Imágenes Libres*

Illustrations: Alfredo Burgos

Layout and Design: Carlos Armando García, based on original
by Oscar William Arce and Miguel Cavada Diez

Library of Congress Cataloging-in-Publication Data
Aguilar Guillén, José Victor.
    [Libre comercio. English]
    Free trade: free rein for transnational corporations / by José Victor Aguilar and Miguel Cavada Diez ; translated by Kathy Ogle.
        p. cm.
    Includes bibliographical references.
    ISBN 0-918346-30-4
    1. Free trade--Latin America. 2. Free Trade Area of the Americas (Organization) I. Cavada Diez, Miguel. II. Title.

HF1745.A36 2003
382'.71--dc21   2003044871

Free Trade: Free Rein for Transnational Corporations

Table of Contents

Index of Tables and Insets

Introduction

We at the *Equipo Maíz* Association in El Salvador have been producing these popular education booklets for 10 years in order to contribute to better understanding, analysis, and debate on topics of importance for grassroots groups in Latin America. This time we've chosen free trade as our topic. We hope this English version will be useful for grassroots organizations in the United States and Canada that are looking critically at free trade and the Free Trade Area of the Americas (FTAA).

In Latin America, we've heard a lot of talk about the FTAA proposed by the United States. We've also heard about the large protests held when governments or international financial institutions have meetings on free trade. In the press, we hear mostly negative things about the protesters. They are called "globophobics" and other things. But we think the protesters have something important to say. More people need to know about how the FTAA will affect the poor in Latin America.

This book addresses three main topics:
1) free trade in general, 2) the FTAA in particular, and 3) the movement against these agreements and against neoliberal globalization.

The main idea of this book is that free trade contains a lot of trade but very little freedom. Free trade, instead of promoting the development of poor countries, is generating extraordinary power and wealth for transnational companies while it sinks most people in poor countries even further into the slavery of poverty.

The protesters aren't the only ones saying that free trade is hurting the poor. International financial institutions themselves know that their policies mostly benefit multinational companies and rich countries.

The World Trade Organization (WTO), for instance, had to create a Center for Technical Assistance to support poor countries in their trade conflicts with developed countries and multinational organizations. Colombia's Minister of Foreign Trade said, "We are seeking a way for globalization and open markets to benefit others in addition to developed countries and multinational businesses." (*La Prensa Gráfica*, October 4, 2001) She knows that most people in poor countries are getting a raw deal. But so far, all of the talks are still headed in the same direction: enrichment for the big companies at the expense of the poor majority.

We are critical of so-called free trade in this book, but we also believe it's important to present policies that *would* be helpful. So, we present some of the proposals coming from civil society groups that want to establish more just trade relations. They want to erradicate poverty and set a higher standard of living for the majority of people in the world.

Finally, we see that "free trade" is not only harming a lot of people in Latin American countries, but it is also hurting poor and working people in places like the United States and Canada just as it enriches a few powerful people and groups in all countries. This book mostly discusses free trade's effect on people in poor countries, but we'd like to hear from working people and grassroots groups in developed countries as well. EPICA, our publishing partner in the United States, can help direct you to places where we can have those conversations, so stay in touch!

Chapter 1

International Trade:
What Does It Have To Do with Me?

I n fact, many of the things we eat, drink, and wear were made in other countries. They are products that have come to our countries through international trade. For example, your TV was probably made in Japan and the movies you watch on it mostly come from the United States.

The diesel fuel that moves the bus we ride comes from a country with oil, like Mexico or Venezuela, and it got here through an oil company like Shell or Texaco. The fertilizer that we put on our corn and bean fields also comes from other countries. The list is endless, but go ahead and see for yourself. Make a list of all the things you use and consume during one day. You'll see that many things you name have come from other countries.

No country in the world can produce everything it needs. That's why the exchange of goods and services is necessary.

Trade is the exchange of goods and services between people and countries. Trade, or commerce, is very important in our lives and for the development of peoples.

No one in the world can say that he or she has nothing to do with trade or commerce. We all take part in commercial activity because we couldn't survive if we didn't exchange goods and services. From the time the sun comes up in the morning until it sets at night, millions of commercial exchanges happen in this country and throughout the world.

If every country produced everything, there would be no need to exchange things, and we could all make everything we need for ourselves. We could sew our own shirts and make our own cars and watches. We could farm the land and feed ourselves. In other words, we could be self-sufficient.

But not every country has the climate to grow all the food products it wants. Not every country has an ocean to get fish. And, unfortunately, we don't all have the machinery and technology to produce what we need to clothe ourselves, feed ourselves, etc.

No one country and no one person can produce everything needed to live. That's why people have to exchange goods and services.

Chapter 2

Key Words Related to International Trade

International trade is the commercial and financial activity that happens between countries.

In this book we look at international trade, that is, commercial transactions between countries. Commercial activity between countries is also called the international market. It's a market where families, businesses, or governments of one country buy and sell to groups in other countries.

The world is a big network of commercial activity. It has a lot of markets and each market has its own rules. Before getting into the topic of free trade, though, we must review some important terms.

Buyers and Sellers

Every country is both a buyer and a seller because not even the most powerful countries have everything. They have to buy the products and services that they don't have and they need to sell the goods and services that they do have. Every country buys and sells. The products one country sells to another are called *exports* and the products it buys from other countries are called *imports*.

For example, El Salvador exports coffee and imports oil. The United States exports cars and imports fruits and vegetables from warmer countries.

We can also think of our household economy in terms of buying and selling. Every month we sell our labor for a salary and with this salary we buy what our family needs.

In world trade not all countries are at the same level. Generally, countries are divided into two categories: industrialized (or developed) countries and developing countries.

Industrialized countries: Industrialized countries have a lot of political and military power and a high level of industrial development that comes from technology. Most of these rich countries are in the northern hemisphere. The seven most industrialized and powerful countries in the world are the USA, Canada, Japan, Germany, England, France, and Italy. They are all in the north. Industrialized countries are also called first world countries.

The industrialized countries are getting richer and richer, and the poor countries are getting poorer.

Developing countries: Although many of these countries are rich in raw materials, they have a lot of problems. They have huge foreign debts, high poverty levels, insufficient industrial development, etc. Most of these countries are in

International trade is controlled by transnational companies.

the southern hemisphere. The poorest countries in the world are in Africa and Latin America. In international organizations, they are not called "poor countries," but Least Developed Countries (LDCs) or, more optimistically, developing countries. They have also been called third world countries.

Freedom To Get Rich

For multinational companies, globalization is very simple. Percy Barnevik, the former president of the multinational electrical equipment company ABB with headquarters in Switzerland, gave the following definition in 1995: "I would define globalization as the freedom for my group of companies to invest where it wants when it wants, to produce what it wants, to buy and sell where it wants, and support the fewest restrictions possible coming from labor laws and social conventions." (Georges Menahen, "Cinco puntos esenciales relativos a las multinacionales," *Le Monde Diplomatique*)

Transnational Corporations

International trade is controlled by the biggest buyers and sellers, transnational corporations from industrialized countries. Transnational, or multinational, corporations are huge companies that do business in many countries of the world. These businesses have a lot of power and they use it to influence the governments of their countries. They usually have the headquarters in the country where the corporation started. Transnational companies produce and control the principal products and services the world economy needs: oil, cars, chemical products, food, telecommunications, etc.

Goods and Services

In all commercial activity something is sold and something is bought. The main goods being bought and sold are *raw materials* (for example, oil, copper, titanium, wood, and cotton.) Raw materials are the basic materials you need to make other things. *Agricultural products* are another kind of good. These are things like wheat, rice, corn, and coffee, products that feed and sustain people.

Manufactured products are also exchanged in the world market. These include computers, cell phones, industrial machinery, and weapons. *Financial products* like money are also bought and sold on the market. Loans, credits, and investments are all financial products.

Services are also bought and sold on the world market. These include health, education, and the transmission of electrical energy.

Of course some goods are much more important than others. These are called *strategic goods*. All countries need these goods. One example is oil. No country can sustain itself today if it doesn't have oil.

Prices

Goods and services have an economic value called *price*. When free competition really exists, the price is fixed according to *the law of supply and demand*. For example, if only a few tons of copper are produced and many countries need it, copper goes up in price. On the other hand, if there is a lot of copper on the market, the price should go down. But in reality, some products are made by only one business. In that case, there is a monopoly instead of free competition, and that business can put any price it wants on its product.

The prices of the main goods and services in international trade are reflected in the *stock market*.

Foreign Exchange

Foreign exchange is the money we need to buy products on the international market. It is the money of the most powerful countries. The main currencies are the U.S. dollar, the Japanese *yen*, and the *euro* from the European Union. You can't get around this one: If you don't have money, you can't buy anything. And if you don't have dollars, *yen,* or *euros*, you can't buy much on the international market.

Protectionism: Tariffs and Non-tariff Trade Barriers

In all commercial activity, both the buyer and the seller try to get the best deal. When you want to buy something, you look for the best quality, appearance, and price. Your goal is to get the best product you can for the least amount of money. The sellers have their own goals too. They want to make the highest profit they can. Their goal is to sell everything they have at a good price for them.

In the international market, the same thing happens but it's more complicated. Every country tries to get an advantage and come out ahead. Each country wants to protect the goods and services it produces. This is called *protectionism.* How is it done? One way is through *tariffs.*

Tariffs are taxes charged to a foreign person or company that wants to sell its products in another country. For example, if a Chilean company wants to sell wine in France, it has to pay a tax to the French government for each bottle of wine it sells. The French government does that to protect French wine producers. If Chileans were able to sell their wine in France more cheaply than the French producers, the French wine makers might soon be out of business.

Tariffs are taxes charged on products that come in from other countries.

Another mechanism used to protect national economies is the *non-tariff trade barrier*. Health regulations are an example. A country might put conditions on certain imported products like meat or grains in order to keep out diseases or harmful insects that could come in through them.

Many governments also protect their national products through *subsidies,* which means they give some sectors economic support for production. The United States, for example, gives millions of dollars in subsidies to its agricultural industry.

Trade Liberalization: Free Trade

For some time now, especially after 1980 with the expansion of neoliberal globalization, efforts have been made to get countries to open up more for trade. They are trying to get rid of tariffs and non-tariff trade barriers so products can be sold more easily in any country.

Free trade demands the elimination of tariffs and trade barriers.

This gets us to the main concept of this book: free trade. In theory, free trade allows all countries to freely buy and sell the goods and services they need. In reality, though, free trade is still a tug-of-war. Each country wants to protect its own products and so it imposes tariffs, but it also wants to sell its products to other countries without having to pay tariffs.

Transnational businesses and the most powerful countries say one thing and do another. They talk about free trade, but they protect their products.

One important problem with "free" trade is that not every country enters the world market on equal terms. Third world countries are rich in raw materials but poor in technology. First world countries or industrialized countries, on the other hand, are rich in technology but they may not be so rich in certain raw materials.

So what happens? Transnational companies influence the governments of their countries to reach agreements that favor their products. In other words, industrialized countries demand that the rest of the world eliminate their tariffs and trade barriers. But they don't practice what they preach at home. The industrialized countries are the first to protect their economies with tariffs and a whole range of trade barriers.

Let's say it another way: If U.S. businesses want to sell computers in Latin America, they try to get all the countries to open their doors and not charge them for selling computers. (This is called trade liberalization.) But if small farmers from a Latin American country want to sell corn to the United States, the U.S. puts up barriers and makes it hard for them to do that. It closes the doors through protectionism in order to protect its own national production of corn.

Chapter 3

The History of Trade in the World

T rade between groups of people didn't begin yesterday. Commercial exchanges have happened between peoples practically since the beginning of humanity. In this chapter we look at the evolution of international trade throughout history.

At first, trade was between neighboring communities, but gradually a more long-distance trade was established.

Commercial Exchange in Primitive Societies

In primitive societies, trade enabled you to get the goods you needed to survive. For example, tribes that mostly raised animals needed to find grains to feed themselves and their animals. When they traded with farming tribes, they exchanged animal hides for goods like wheat or potatoes. At first the exchange was direct, product for product (for example, trading one sheep for one hundred pounds of wheat). Later, things like fish, salt, and cattle were used as money. The Pipil Indians of Central America used *cacao* seeds as money for their commercial activities. Later they used precious metals like gold and silver. Today we use paper money, checks, credit cards, and electronic signals.

Navigation and Colonialism

At first, trade happened between neighboring communities, but gradually long-distance trade developed. That gave rise to a group of people who specialized in trade. That's how traders, or *merchants*, came to be. They started accumulating wealth and many of them became capitalists.

World trade increased as sea travel developed. Explorers like Christopher Columbus and Vasco de Gama were looking for new ocean routes to gain access to spices from other parts of the world. Soon, powerful countries were sailing to other countries, conquering them, and taking their spices, gold, and other things of value. That's how colonization began. The powerful countries became empires. They divided up the world into colonies and started taking all the wealth out of the colonies that "belonged" to them. This wealth was the basis for the development of the capitalist system. The countries that are called developed countries today got their start back then.

Industrialization and the Theory of Trade

The invention of the steam engine and the development of land and air transportation gave rise to the growth of large industries where products were produced in large quantities on assembly lines. From then on, goods were produced, not to satisfy the direct needs of the people who produced them, but rather as a way to generate more profit for capitalists.

With capitalist production, classical economists like British David Ricardo started talking about *comparative advantage*. This trade theory said that each country or region should specialize in the products it was best equipped to produce, that is, products that it could produce more efficiently, more cheaply, and with better quality than any other country or region.

This served as a base for the *international division of labor* that allowed some countries to specialize in industrial goods and other countries to specialize in raw materials or agricultural goods.

For many
years trade
policies
protected
national
products.

For many years, most countries tried to *protect national production*. This meant that they charged tariffs on foreign products or they put up non-tariff barriers like quota systems or health regulations. Rich countries still apply these measures to develop their industries and limit the entry of products from other countries.

Trade in Latin America from the 1950s to the 1970s

From the 1950s to the 1970s, an *Import Substitution* strategy was promoted in Latin America to support industrialization. The idea was to encourage national businesses to produce more goods and services rather than buy them from other countries through imports. Another part of the strategy was to open more markets in neighboring countries and to promote regional trade agreements like the Central American Common Market and the Andean Pact.

The regional markets protected themselves from competition from other countries and trade blocks through a *common external tariff.* That meant that all the countries that signed the regional agreement had to charge the same taxes on products coming in from other parts of the world.

Neoliberal globalization proposes more open or "free" trade. This will make it harder for small producers to sell many of their products.

Neoliberal Policies and the Domination of Transnational Companies

When neoliberal economics became dominant in the 1980s, *open market* policies were emphasized. These policies supported eliminating all barriers to trade (like taxes and tariffs) and having no restrictions on the circulation of money in poor countries. This approach favored the large transnational corporations, who quickly began to move in to Latin America.

In this new context, strategies of regional cooperation have been quickly replaced by bilateral or multilateral free trade agreements that are based on promoting the free circulation of goods and foreign capital.

Today people don't talk about comparative advantage as much as *competitive advantage,* which comes from taking advantage of technological and scientific advances and skilled labor. Getting the most out of trade doesn't depend only on material resources, climate, and geographic location; it also depends on technology and knowledge. For example, a country that has oil but not the equipment needed to extract the oil from the ground, needs the technology of transnational businesses like Shell or Texaco to get the oil out.

Now people talk about competitive advantage rather than comparative advantage.

The groups that are in the best position to make the most out of these advantages are large transnational corporations and rich countries who have control of the technological advances, financial resources, and research and development capacity. In many cases, these competitive advantages depend on finding places that can offer cheap labor and don't require much protection for workers.

International Trade, Wars, and Embargoes

International trade is not just an economic activity. It's also a political and military reality. Most conflicts and wars have a trade issue behind them: the control of some strategic product or the ability to dominate the market of a certain region.

For example, the mineral *columbite tantalite,* also known as *coltan,* is a little-known but strategic material used to make ballistic missiles and cell phones, among other things. Most of the known reserves of this mineral are in Africa, especially in the mines of the Kivu region inside the Democratic Republic of the Congo. During a genocidal war in that region, Ugandan and Rwandan armies occupied the area surrounding the mines in order to keep extracting the mineral for sale to companies in the United States and other places. According to the United Nations, illegal traffic in coltan was one of the causes of the war. More than two million people were killed between 1997 and 2001 before the United States took action and got the armies to pull out. (While the September 11 attacks in the United States received huge amounts of coverage by press and by businesses, the conflict in the Congo received very little coverage.)

Most conflicts and wars in the world have been over trade issues.

Trade can also be used as a tool of war. One example is the economic embargo imposed by the United States against Cuba for the last 40 years. This embargo is a way to punish Cuba for rejecting the capitalist system.

Chapter 4

The World Trade Organization (WTO)

T he World Trade Organization (WTO) is a global institution with a huge role in trade.

How the World Trade Organization Began

After World War II, three institutions were created that became very influential in the world economic system:

- The International Bank for Reconstruction and Development (better known as the World Bank) was to be in charge of providing money to rebuild countries destroyed by the war.

- The International Monetary Fund (IMF) was given the task of ensuring the stability of the international monetary system.

- The General Agreement on Tariffs and Trade (GATT) was put in charge of eliminating trade barriers.

Years later, the GATT became the World Trade Organization. The GATT was just a treaty, and it wasn't strong enough to enforce its own agreements. A long series of negotiations called the Uruguay Round began in September 1986 in Uruguay and ended in April 1994 in Morocco. The World Trade Organization was created from these negotiations.

The Objectives of the WTO and How It Works

The World Trade Organization is made up of representatives of the governments of 142 countries. China was recently approved to be a member. On its web page the WTO says it is the "only global international organization dealing with the rules of trade between nations" and that its goal is "to help producers of goods and services, exporters, and importers conduct their business." It also says that its objective is the well-being of the populations of its member countries.

The World Trade Organization makes the rules that govern international trade.

From time to time the WTO holds assemblies so the representatives of the various member countries can negotiate new trade agreements. The last assembly was held in No-

Free trade is opening the borders of countries so that products and money can circulate throughout the world with absolute freedom.

vember 2001 in Doha, Qatar, where an agenda was approved for a new round of negotiations.

Often these negotiations are difficult because each country is defending its own interests. For example, the 1999 assembly held in Seattle was a total failure. Several countries refused to sign the agreement because they felt it was being imposed on them. They hadn't even had time to read it.

Transnational company executives are often behind the scenes pressuring government representatives to sign agreements favorable to their own economic interests.

Criticisms of the WTO

The WTO has been criticized for many things including the following:

The WTO is an instrument of neoliberal globalization.

The WTO, the World Bank, and the International Monetary Fund are sometimes called the "pagan trinity" because these three powerful international organizations promote and direct the entire process of neoliberal globalization. They are like gods who decide the economic policies for the whole world. Many people believe these organizations do exactly what the transnational companies tell them to do.

The World Bank, the IMF, and the WTO are called the "pagan trinity" because they have so much decision-making power.

Free Trade Is a Fairy Tale

What is free trade? I think it's a fairy tale. Because as far as I can tell it only means that huge mega-businesses get more and more control over production, services, domestic and international trade, finances, strategic resources, communications, and information. Businesses get bigger by merging with each other and their only goal is to make a profit. They don't want to have any responsibility for the social consequences of this or for the stability of nations.

If you look at how free trade works, you'll find some surprises. For example, Japan allows only 5% foreign investment in its country. Ninety-five percent of the financial system and 95% of investments in Japan are Japanese. So, financial free trade doesn't exist in Japan. Of course, Japan opens its borders for products against which they are already highly competitive. They tell US investors, "Come. Our doors are open to you. Bring in your cars etc." China, where a fifth of the world's population lives, had the highest growth rate in the world over the last 20 years. But in China, 92% of investments are owned by the State. They allow only 8% foreign investment and half of that has to be by Chinese people who live out of the country. So free trade doesn't exist in China either.

In the European Union only 14% of the cars that circulate in Europe come from outside of Europe. 86% of car production is European. According to law, fifty-one percent of what is called audiovisual space (movies, TV, radio, news, advertisements etc.) has to be European, too. And sixty five percent of all exports and imports from the European Union are based on agreements where Europe will buy only from countries they can sell to. They don't have a totally open economy either.

These statistics show that in reality, the free trade they are selling us is only for Latin America, what's left of Africa, part of Russia (at least until the recent crisis set in because now they're turning back the clock), and a few other places. The long and short of it is that free trade is a policy being forced on us. (Alcira Argumedo, "*Pobreza y desigualdad social en el MERCOSUR*," *BuenosAiresOculta*, August 25, 2001)

The WTO allows subsidies that favor the rich.

A subsidy is economic assistance that a government gives to certain private businesses or economic activities to help them compete in the international market. For example, the French government gives aid to its farmers. If it weren't for these subsidies, French agricultural products would be more expensive and they couldn't compete with other countries on the world market.

Subsidies don't happen the same everywhere. The governments of the United States and the European Union invest millions of dollars to subsidize (help) certain private businesses and economic activities in their countries but they insist that other governments eliminate *their* subsidies! To date, the WTO has not managed to reach an agreement on this topic. As the old saying goes, "either it's fair for everybody or it's not fair for anybody." If the United States can subsidize its products, why can't India or any other country do the same?

According to the theory of free trade, subsidies should disappear because they distort the market. Why? Because a company that gets a government subsidy can make its product cheaper than a company that does not.

To make countries more equal, poor countries should be allowed to give more subsidies to their industries. Instead, the rich countries keep subsidizing their industries and the poor nations can't compete.

The WTO has not eliminated dumping.

Another criticism of the World Trade Organization is that it hasn't eliminated *dumping*. Dumping happens when a company exports a product at a price lower than the price it normally charges in its own country. Companies do this in order to undersell their competition and drive them out of business. For example, the United States steel industry practices dumping so that its steel can be cheaper than the steel of other countries

Sometimes dumping is when a company cuts workers' salaries or benefits in order to reduce production costs. This is how the company can put its products on the market at a cheaper rate than anyone else can. Businesses dump their products on the world market by sacrificing workers' rights.

Dumping is an unfair practice that contradicts the idea of free trade for two reasons: 1) it keeps competition from happening on equal ground, and 2) it hurts the rights of workers all over the world.

Dumping involves lowering the costs of your products by sacrificing the fair wages and labor rights of your workers.

The WTO is rigid about intellectual property rights and patents.

When a person or company invents a new product, the first thing they do is patent it. Patenting is a legal process that makes the person or the company the owner of the product idea. That means that if other people or companies want to make that same product, they have to pay the owner first. The patent means that the product idea is the "intellectual property" of the inventor.

There are several problems with patents and intellectual property rights. For example, if a government wants to make a medicine to treat an illness in its country, it has to buy the rights to do that from the transnational company that first patented the formula for the medicine. Also, patents on medicines make prices go up, which makes many medicines inaccessible to consumers in poor countries. This puts the health of millions of people at risk.

Brazil has been trying to increase its own production of medicines to treat AIDS. But the United States is not happy about this and is trying to stop it by increasing protection for intellectual property rights at the World Trade Organization. The same thing happened with South Africa when it passed a law in 1997 to make AIDS medications more accessible to its population. More than four million people are affected by the AIDS virus in South

Protection for Patents

Curiously, this is the only agreement of the World Trade Organization that calls for more state protectionism at a time when we are immersed in a wave of liberalizations. Why is it that they don't liberalize the patents and allow them to circulate freely in the world? In 1995, industrialized countries had 97 percent of all of the patents in the world. And more than half of all patent fees have been paid to the United States. (Joaquín García and Juan Velásquez, "Reflexiones sobre la OMC," *Cultura de la Esperanza.* www.rebelion.org/economia/htm August 23, 2000)

Africa. But the transnational companies that own the patents on the medicines sued the South African government for trying to go around intellectual property rights to provide cheaper medicines. Recently there have been some court rulings against these transnationals but for the most part, intellectual property rights continue to be protected by free trade agreements in spite of problems with their rigid application.

***The WTO allows free transit for goods and money but not
for people.***

"Free" trade is not being applied to labor. Goods and capital
(money) can cross borders without any problem, but people who
seek better living conditions in another country face enormous
difficulties and obstacles to crossing the borders.

If a company wants to take money from one country to another,
there's no problem. The doors are open. If a company wants to
sell televisions or cell phones in another country, there's no problem there either. But if a worker wants to go to another country
where he or she can earn more in wages, the borders are closed.
In free trade, freedom is only for money and goods, not for people.

WTO policies increase inequality and poverty.

Another criticism of World Trade Organization policies is that free trade has not contributed to reducing poverty in the world as promised. It has, in fact, done the opposite.

Labor Market Flexibility

> International economic agreements called "free trade agreements" are basically designed to maintain the status quo. One of the elements of these agreements is what they call "labor market flexibility." [Free trade proponents] demand that all barriers to labor mobility and salary flexibility be eliminated. But what does that mean? It doesn't mean that workers can be free to go where they want—that Mexican workers could go to New York, for example. What it means is that they can be freely fired from their jobs. They want to take away barriers to kicking people *out* of their jobs. And salary flexibility means flexibility for salaries to be reduced, not increased. (Noam Chomsky, "The Meaning of Seattle" interview with David Barsamian in *Z Magazine*)

Free trade has not contributed to reducing poverty in the world.

Some people say that thanks to free trade, economic prosperity has been extended to all of the countries in the world. Every day more people have access to a higher standard of living: the latest car, comfortable housing, vacations on the beach, cable TV, name-brand clothing, and personal computers. They can choose which private school they want for their children, which private hospital they can go to if they are sick, which retirement fund they are going to invest in, etc. According to this view, free trade has opened the door of happiness and well-being for thousands and thousands of families. The daily media coverage contributes to this image of the "happy world" created by free trade.

Statistics on the Social and Economic Situation of the World

POPULATION

6 billion people live on the planet.

1.15 billion people live in the northern industrialized countries.

4.62 billion people live in the south, also called poor or developing countries.

HUNGER

800 million people suffer from chronic malnutrition.

200 million children under the age of 5 are malnourished.

11 million children die every year from malnutrition.

POVERTY

1.6 billion people are worse off than they were 15 years ago.

1.4 billion people (one-quarter of the world's population) live below the poverty level.

A half a billion women live in extreme poverty.

1.3 billion people live on less than $1 a day: 110 million of these are in the Americas, 970 million in Asia, and 200 million in Africa.

DEVELOPMENT

89 countries are worse off economically than they were 10 years ago.

70 countries have less income than they had during the decades of the 1960s and 1970s.

ILLITERACY

One billion people are illiterate. Of these, 600 million are women.

HEALTH AND POTABLE WATER

The south has an average of one doctor for every 6000 people. The north has one for every 350 people.

One billion people live without potable water.

Statistics from the Movimento de Resistencia Global-Praga 2000, Catalunya

The Richest People Keep Getting Richer

"The two-hundred richest people keep getting richer. The net worth of these 200 people grew from 440 billion dollars in 1994 to 1.042 trillion dollars in 1998. Today these fortunes are more than the total income of 41% of the entire population of the world." (United Nations Development Program 1999, cited by UNIFEM, *The Progress of Women in the World, 2000*)

But only a half billion people can access this comfortable life. And six billion people live on this planet! For 5.5 billion of the world's people the doors and windows of progress and happiness are closed and sealed. It is true that world policies of free trade have increased income and wealth, but only for a few people!!

The following statistic is scandalous: The combined fortunes of the 200 richest people in the world are greater than the total income of almost half of the world's population (2.46 billion people)!

World Trade Organization policies have made the rich richer and the poor poorer. Because of this, an expert on the topic concludes that the majority of the population is excluded from the market:

Free trade benefits a half a billion people, but there are 6 billion of us on this planet.

> The idea that this economic prosperity has been extended all over the world is a myth. It's a fairy tale with a happy ending that has very little to do with

reality. The immense majority of the population is not included in this system of consumption and sales because they can't afford to be consumers. Rather, they are poised to join the silent statistics of those 30 million people who die of hunger every year. (Pedro Pérez Ramírez, "La globalización y la resistencia contra el neoliberalismo," Colectivo CRALED, *Cuaderno de Materiales de Ensayo*. May 15, 2001)

Chapter 5.

Trade Blocks

T he current tendency is for countries from the same region to join together in trade blocks to control the market in their region and to have more power than countries in another region. Many bilateral agreements (agreements between just two countries) are also signed.

In this chapter we discuss the principal trade blocks, especially one being negotiated now: the Free Trade Area of the Americas.

Trade Blocks

Trade blocks seek to integrate the economies of countries in a particular region.

Trade blocks seek to integrate the economies of countries in the same region. They eliminate trade barriers and other obstacles to investments between participating countries. It's as if that region didn't have any borders, economically speaking, and became just one country. In that way, their market is bigger and they can combine efforts to protect themselves from products that come from other regions or trade blocks.

Some existing trade blocks are the North American Free Trade Agreement (NAFTA), the European Union, and the Southeast Asian Block. Pages 52 and 53 show the primary trade blocks and the countries in them. Not all the member countries of a trade block have the same power. One or two countries usually have the leadership and get more benefits from the trade agreement.

Free Trade Area of the Americas (FTAA)

The United States proposed the idea of the FTAA and would like to have it in place by 2005. Negotiations for this trade agreement are just beginning, but we can already see the enormous repercussions it would have in the countries of Latin America.

The Goals and Reach of the FTAA

The FTAA is a trade agreement that would include everything from Alaska to the *Tierra del Fuego* in southern Argentina, that is, the whole length of North, Central, and South America. If it were passed, it would be the largest trade block in the world with 800 million people. The FTAA began to be promoted at the First Summit of the Americas, held in Miami in 1994.

The United States proposed the idea of the FTAA and would like to have it in place by 2005.

The Main Trade Blocks in the World

North American Free Trade Agreement (NAFTA)

United States
Canada
Mexico

The Central American Common Market

Guatemala   El Salvador
Honduras   Nicaragua
Costa Rica

The Central American Common Market is not in good shape because each country has made its own (unilateral) decisions. For example, Costa Rica and Nicaragua each signed free trade agreements with Mexico separately, and the "Northern Triangle" countries of Guatemala, Honduras, and El Salvador signed another agreement with Mexico that took effect in January 2001.

The Andean Community

Venezuela   Colombia
Bolivia   Ecuador
Peru

The South American Common Market (MERCOSUR)

Brazil   Argentina
Chile   Uruguay
Paraguay

The Caribbean Economic Community

Antigua   Barbados
Barbuda   Granada
The Bahamas   Santa Lucia
Belize   Surinam
Haiti   Dominican Republic
St. Vincent   The Granadinas
St. Kitts   Trinidad and Tobago
Dominica

Trade blocks are geographical and territorial. They are trade agreements between countries in the same geographic zone or region. NAFTA and MERCOSUR are both examples of trade blocks.

At the same time, there are **trade agreements** between countries that are not in the same geographic zone. These treaties can be bilateral (between two countries) or multilateral (between several countries).

Sometimes a country from a certain trade block negotiates a trade agreement with a country outside its trade block. For example, Chile belongs to MERCOSUR, but it also has its own trade agreements with other countries like the United States.

The European Union (EU)

Germany	Denmark
France	Greece
Italy	England
Spain	Austria
Portugal	Sweden
Holland	Ireland
Belgium	Finland
Luxembourg	

This block is the most integrated. They even have a single currency: the Euro.

The South East Asian Block

Japan	Vietnam
Singapore	Philippines
Malaysia	Cambodia
Taiwan	Brunei
Hong Kong	Mayanmar (Burma)
Indonesia	South Korea

In this block, South Korea, Singapore, Taiwan, and Hong Kong are called the "Asian Tigers" because they are the newly industrialized countries of Asia.

In April 2001 another Summit of the Americas was held in Canada and the FTAA was on the agenda. At that time they said, "the central objective of the Free Trade Agreement of the Americas is to reduce poverty and strengthen democracy." They went as far as to say that the goal would be to "cut in half the number of people living in poverty in the Americas before the year 2015." But if past experience with free trade is any example, poverty will increase, not decrease, with the FTAA.

The Scope of the FTAA Negotiations

"These negotiations have an immense scope. They include tariff reductions for manufactured products and natural resource products. They include protections for investors and intellectual property rights. They include rules on government purchases and on subsidies to agricultural producers. The FTAA negotiations will also include conversations about services that affect practically all aspects of human activity, from birth to funerals, from maintenance of local systems of water distribution and sewage to speculation on world financial markets, from basic primary education to research and advanced scientific development." (Public Services International, *Democracy or Dominance in the Americas? The FTAA Versus Public Services*. www.world-psi.org)

Questions about the FTAA

Grassroots organizations of the poor have seriously questioned the FTAA because it is a neoliberal project that glorifies "the free market" and benefits large transnational companies. The transnationals are given all kinds of breaks in this proposed agreement: Government property is turned over to them through privatizations. They get power over governments. They can even bankrupt government businesses, generating more unemployment and poverty and increasing the size of the informal sector.

One of the most controversial points is the FTAA chapter on investments, which looks a lot like Chapter Eleven of the North American Free Trade Agreement (NAFTA). This chapter says that transnational companies can sue governments and demand compensation if those governments don't comply with certain obligations of the agreement. In other words, transnational corporations are given more power than governments.

The FTAA chapter on investments gives transnational corporations more power than governments.

According to the Hemispheric Social Alliance, "This unprecedented power authorized to corporations restricts the ability of governments to protect public well-being and the environment and their ability to assure that investments are made in a way that helps meet the social and economic development objectives of the people."

The FTAA is part of the "America for Americans" strategy, which really means "America for the United States and its transnational corporations." The objective of the FTAA is to ensure U.S. trade domination on both American continents.

NAFTA Examples That Set Precedents for the FTAA

When the Canadian government tried to outlaw a toxic fuel additive called MMT, the U.S.-based Ethyl Corporation that makes MMT successfully sued the government of Canada for $13 million in damages. The Canadian government was forced to withdraw its prohibition of MMT, even though it is a known toxin that attacks the human nervous system. The Canada-based Ethyl Corporation then sued the state of California for prohibiting MBTE, another toxic fuel additive, and demanded the sum of $970 million.

U.S.-based Metalclad Corporation took a Mexican state to court for not allowing the company to put a toxic waste dump in its territory, arguing that environmental zoning by the state was equivalent to expropriation. (ATTAC-Mendoza, *The FTAA In Synthesis*)

The FTAA's political objective is to isolate Cuba for maintaining a political system not approved by the United States. This is why Cuba is left out of the FTAA negotiations.

What Do Transnational Corporations Have to Gain from Such Poor Countries?

Some people ask, "What can big corporations from countries like the United States gain from countries as poor as El Salvador where the great majority of people don't have any purchasing power?" We must remember that the United States doesn't see El Salvador or other poor countries as just places to sell its products, but also as resources for lowering its costs of production.

In addition to taking advantage of the purchasing power of the countries' middle and upper classes, transnational businesses are also looking for cheap labor and natural resources so they can make their products. They are also looking for countries with low taxes and few environmental or other regulations and controls.

For example, it's cheaper for a U.S. shoe factory to make shoes in El Salvador than in the United States. Of course, that business will try to sell some of its shoes in El Salvador, but it is more interested in using Salvadoran labor to produce shoes more cheaply.

Conclusion

If the FTAA agreement is signed, it will become the largest trade block in the world. Some people and organizations think that this will help resolve the problems of poverty in Latin American countries. Others, however, think that the FTAA will be a way for the United States and its transnational corporations to dominate the American continents.

Chapter 6

Trade Agreements and Their Impact on Women

Economic problems in the world can't be reduced simply to inequalities between rich and poor. Another serious issue must be taken into account: Poverty in the world affects women more than men. We must ask ourselves: Do the agreements that the World Trade Organization promotes contribute to overcoming the inequality between men and women and reducing the exclusion and marginalization of women? In this chapter we look at trade agreements from the perspective of women.

Women's Work at Home Is not Recognized

Domestic work is not bought or sold on the international market.

The domestic work and child care that most women are involved in doesn't produce goods that can be bought or sold. So women's domestic work is not taken into account in trade negotiations and agreements. But this isn't all. This kind of "women's work" isn't even taken into account in national economic data. In spite of the fact that women work everyday from sunup to sundown (and more), officially they don't do anything. Let's look at this more closely.

Statistics show that domestic work is done primarily by women. There are two problems with this. The first problem is that the work is not paid. Women cook food, wash and iron clothes, clean house, take care of the health and the education of the family group, etc. This work doesn't have a quitting time, it doesn't come with vacation, and it's not paid. Since it doesn't generate any income, it is not seen as having any value for the country's economy.

The other problem is that the product that women make is invisible. Women who do multiple tasks in their homes don't generate products that you can see, touch, or trade inside or outside the country. They don't produce watches or televisions or any other product. They produce healthier, cleaner, more cared-for family members who then become workers in the economy, but economists who look at international trade don't give this work any importance.

In addition to doing domestic work, many women also work outside the home to increase the income of their family. Most women work in the informal sector, selling little things on the street or from their homes. In developing countries, if you look around at who does this kind of informal work, you will see that the majority are women.

The majority of women work in the informal sector, which isn't included as a factor in international trade.

But does the fact that hundreds of women sell clothing or fruit in the center of town mean anything for international trade? Absolutely not, because it's an activity only for an internal market.

A large part of the economic activity that women engage in (domestic work, sales, etc.) is not seen as connected with international trade. Because of this, trade agreements don't accurately understand many women's economic lives and they don't offer adequate solutions for women who are doing double or triple duty at home and in the workplace.

The Massive Influx of Foreign Products

WTO trade agreements promote a massive entry of products made by large multinational companies into developing countries from other countries. They are products of all kinds from toothbrushes, clothing, and shoes, to medicines and canned

foods. The main result of this is that local businesses go bankrupt because they can't compete with giant companies that have more money and technology. When local businesses go bankrupt, unemployment increases.

Unemployment affects women more than men, no matter who in the family is laid off, because women are the ones who go the extra mile to find income for the family by going into the informal sector. As national businesses go under, the informal sector swells, and the majority of people in the informal sector are women.

Worsening Working Conditions

International competition has also worsened working conditions. How is this explained? It's simple. Many companies, national or international, reduce their payrolls to compete with other companies and sell their products. As needed, they'll contract someone for a short period of time rather than pay a permanent fulltime worker. So neither women nor men have much job security. Today they have a job, but tomorrow who knows? Businesses also bust unions and they lower wages and benefits to be competitive. Governments turn a blind eye to these things arguing that it is better to have a bad job than no job at all. Women are the most affected by this deterioration in working conditions because they have lower-paid, more precarious jobs to begin with.

A clear example is work at assembly-for-export plants or *maquilas*, where the majority of employees are women. Women are forced to take these jobs in spite of the fact that they have to work under great pressure to meet company production goals, and in spite of the fact that pay is sometimes lower than the legal minimum wage. They work in conditions of poor health and

Women who work in maquilas *do so in terrible working conditions.*

Cuts in social spending increase the burden of women's work at home.

hygiene, and sometimes they are mistreated. Why would they work in such conditions? The company and the government remind them that they have no choice: "Take it or leave it," they say. "There are lines of people waiting outside for this job." Companies take advantage of women's abysmal situation of poverty to exploit them even further.

Cuts in Social Spending

Another reason that international trade agreements impact women is that governments are asked to reduce social spending. Social spending is money the government spends to improve the living conditions of its population, especially in health and education. To get the money to construct hospitals, promote health campaigns, improve education, build roads, and increase public services like access to water, the government has to charge taxes.

Some of these taxes come from the tariffs charged on foreign imports.

Since WTO agreements are made under the principal of opening up trade, governments have to commit to lower or eliminate taxes on imports of foreign products. As a consequence, the stores fill up with foreign products, but the government has less income. Faced with this situation, governments take simple measures: They reduce social spending, raise the prices on public services, and increase the kind of taxes that hurt the poor the most (like sales taxes and value added taxes).

Cuts in Social spending increase the burden for women in their homes.

So the price of water goes up, the public hospitals start charging for appointments, and people have to struggle harder to get medicines. In addition, salaries are often frozen for public servants like teachers. Who pays the highest price? Women. If the government cuts social spending, the family's economic situation worsens. Women must then dedicate more time to help make ends meet. They increase their work burden even further, taking away the little time they might have had for personal development.

Conclusion

International trade agreements unleash a series of events that end up impacting women negatively at the level of their daily lives.

Chapter 7

The Movement Against Unfair and Unequal Trade

The World Trade Organization, the World Bank, the International Monetary Fund, and the Inter-American Development Bank are all part of the neoliberal model of globalization that is generating more poverty and exclusion in large sectors of humanity. Because of this, they now face large demonstrations of people who reject this model. Opposition is coming from many social sectors as well as from governments of some poor countries who are WTO members.

The Anti-Globalization Movement

The people in social protest movements against neoliberal globalization have been called "globophobics."

The movement against this kind of globalization is made up of a wide range of citizens and organizations: students, human rights groups, non-governmental organizations, women's groups, ecologists, etc. The anti-globalization movement is present in many countries of the industrialized world. Its members communicate on the Internet and even though they are not invited, they go where the international organizations hold their meetings in order to protest and to present their proposals.

Those who benefit from globalization have a negative view of the anti-globalization movement, and the media usually presents the movement in a less than flattering light. They call the people who participate "globophobics," insinuating that they are naively afraid of globalization.

In reality, the people who participate in this movement are not opposed to globalization; they are opposed to the way globalization is happening. They are opposed to the neoliberal economic model that concentrates wealth and power in the hands of transnational corporations and causes more poverty in the world.

The social movement against neoliberal globalization has been the most visible in the massive protests held in the places where the international financial organizations like the WTO, the World Bank, and the IMF have had their meetings. These institutions and some governments are now looking at ways to have their summits and meetings at sea or on military bases so that the demonstrators can't get close.

Women's Protests

Women's groups and networks of women's organizations all over the world are playing a very active role in the anti-globalization movement because neoliberal globalization is generating more social inequalities, especially between men and women. Women have demonstrated against the WTO and against the FTAA, among other things.

The Biggest Protests of the Anti-Globalization Movement

Seattle, Washington
November 1999
The Third Ministerial Conference of the WTO

This was supposed to have been the "Summit of the Millennium." More than 40,000 demonstrators protested against the powerful organizations that were negotiating at the summit. Invited officials from several countries also showed their discontent by refusing to sign some of the agreements.

In heated discussions, the United States, Japan, and member countries of the European Union accused each other of not complying with the free trade agreements that they had made.

Cancun, Mexico
March 2001
The World Economic Forum

The anti-globalization movement was present and made its voice heard.

Washington D.C.
April 2000
Meetings of the World Bank and the IMF

Demonstrators called the World Bank, the IMF, and the WTO the "pagan trinity," instruments of globalization that are further impoverishing poor countries. They also stated that the "large corporations who exploit the raw materials of the third world are producing enormous human and environmental costs."

**Prague, the Czech Republic
September 2000**
Meetings of the World Bank
and the IMF

Several protest demonstrations occurred.

**Davos , Switzerland
January 2001**
The World Economic Forum

The anti-globalization movement demonstrated in the streets of Davos in protest.

The chief economist at the World Bank, Joseph Stiglitz, stated that free trade had benefited poor countries little or not at all, and that the theory of free trade was "intellectual fraud." Shortly afterward he left the World Bank.

**Quebec, Canada
April 2001**
The Summit of the Americas

Presidents of countries on the American continents discussed an agreement proposed by the United States: the Free Trade Agreement of the Americas (FTAA).

The meeting organizers put up an enormous fence to keep protesters from getting close to the meeting. But the protesters knocked it down and let their opposition be heard.

**Genoa, Italy
March 2001**
Meeting of the Group of Seven

The presidents of the seven richest and most powerful countries of the world met. (The United States, England, Germany, Canada, France, Italy, and Japan)

Protests were violently repressed, causing the death of one of the protesters.

Women are asking for their agenda to be incorporated into international trade negotiations.

Women's groups are demanding that the institutions that promote trade and globalization incorporate a gender analysis into their work. They are also demanding the implementation of agreements reached in international conferences on gender equity. For example, many women's groups are asking that the agreements from the 1995 Beijing Conference on Women be made into law.

Conclusion

Neoliberal economics is not the only thing that is globalizing. We are also seeing a growing globalization of protests and solidarity. A growing network of grassroots and non-governmental groups from the majority of countries has made its voice of opposition and protest heard in the international financial organizations that make economic and political decisions. These international organizations and some of the governments are trying to make this movement look bad. They say it is just a small group of troublemakers.

Chapter 8

Proposals for Fair International Trade

Eradication of Poverty	Gradual Elimination of Trade Barriers		Development for Women
Redistribution of Wealth		Regulation and Control of Speculative Capital	Preservation and Restoration of the Environment
Respect for Cultures and Ethnic Identities	Respect for Human Rights		Protection of Biodiversity
Respect for the Sovereignty of Nations		Citizen Participation in Negotiating Trade Agreements	Cancellation of the Foreign Debt

T he anti-globalization movement is not just about protest. It's also about coming up with alternative proposals for an international system based on human development, a system where people—not goods, money, or profit—are at the center of all economy and trade.

The proposals of the anti-globalization movement have been discussed and debated in many major meetings like the World Social Forum and the Peoples' Summits. In this chapter we review the primary proposals.

The Peoples' Summits

The Peoples' Summits are spaces where grassroots and social organizations of the Americas meet to discuss and create alternatives to the FTAA and other trade agreements in the American continents. There have been two summits: the first in Santiago, Chile, in 1998 and the second in Quebec in 2001 (at exactly the same place and time that the presidents were meeting to negotiate the FTAA at the Summit of the Americas). There will be a third People's Summit in April 2003 in Argentina.

Eradication of Poverty

International trade currently favors the development of countries that are already developed. Because of this, the primary proposal of the fair trade movement is to make the well-being of *all* people of the world a central objective. Trade should also strengthen the production capacity of each country, especially the poorest ones. Trade should generate employment and should be oriented toward eradicating two of the worst problems of humanity: poverty and marginalization, both of which affect millions of people today.

Gradual Elimination of Trade Barriers

If the WTO-proposed elimination of trade barriers were to happen all at once everywhere without distinction, the strongest countries and corporations would be the winners in a winner-take-all game, worsening the inequalities that already exist. The alternative proposal is for a gradual elimination of trade barriers so the poorest countries can strengthen their national production and have more favorable conditions in which to compete in the international market.

World Social Forums

The World Social Forums have been held in Brazil in January 2001, 2002, and 2003. In these meetings, thousands of representatives of grassroots and social movements from all over the world met together with other grassroots leaders and intellectuals committed to building alternatives to neoliberalism. The World Social Forum is a response to the World Economic Forum, where big bankers and presidents of transnational companies meet with representatives of the international financial organizations that promote neoliberal globalization.

Development for Women

When international trade agreements are signed, the reality of women's lives is ignored. The anti-globalization movement proposes that international trade agreements should include the various commitments that many countries have made, but not implemented, to aid women's development. Trade agreements should give priority to eliminating inequality between men and women, and to improving working conditions in the *maquilas*.

Redistribution of Wealth

Where there is trade, there is profit. But how are those profits distributed? International trade as it's now being promoted by neoliberal globalization concentrates wealth in the hands of a few, and especially in the hands of transnational corporations and in small groups of businesspeople in each country.

The alternative movement says that the wealth generated by international commerce should be distributed fairly within countries and between countries. How? Through taxes. Those who have more should pay more in taxes, and those taxes should be invested in improving the living conditions of lower-income people.

Regulation and Control of Speculative Capital

Speculative capital is money that is not invested in production. This money goes from country to country and from bank to bank, looking for better interest rates. If international trade rules change to remove all controls and barriers to this type of capital, powerful people will take the shortest and surest way out. Instead of investing their money in their country to strengthen agriculture or industry, they'll take it out of the country and invest it in a bank that pays them interest just for having their money there. This kind of wealth creates more wealth, but only for the people who already have money.

One of the proposals is to charge a tax on international financial transactions.

The alternative movement is in favor of international trade agreements that establish some control and regulation on this type of capital. For example, it proposes a tax on entry of all speculative capital and on the repatriation of profits. This tax is called a Tobin Tax, because James Tobin, a Nobel Prize winning economist, proposed it.

Some people calculate that a 0.1% tax applied to the monthly total of all financial transactions between countries would generate $230 trillion every year. This money could be used toward satisfying the basic needs of millions of people in poverty. French officials are considering proposing such a tax in the European Union.

Preservation and Restoration of the Environment

Trade agreements should not be based on the unlimited exploitation of natural resources.

Trade agreements should not undermine environmental commitments. The destruction of the ozone layer by the emission of toxic gasses, the destruction of the Amazon jungle, and the contamination of rivers and oceans are very serious problems that put human life in jeopardy. Trade agreements and treaties should not be based on the limitless exploitation of natural resources. We need to restore and care for the environment.

Protection of Biodiversity

Big corporations are now genetically altering seeds, producing genetically modified organisms or GMOs. This is dangerous for two reasons: 1) farmers will have to buy new seeds every year from big companies like Monsanto instead of saving the seeds from their own harvest to plant the following year, and 2) the genetically altered plants can quickly interbreed with other plants and destroy native plant varieties that are more resistant to drought and plagues.

Corporations are also making certain life forms subject to private ownership, and they are converting life sources into products that can generate wealth and power. If corporations have their way, even things like medicinal plants that people have used for centuries will be patented and sold. People who don't have enough money won't be able to buy them. Grassroots and social justice organizations say that biodiversity belongs to all humanity, and that no trade agreement should keep humanity from accessing the wealth of biodiversity. Instead, trade agreements should do the opposite! They should protect biodiversity because it is fundamental to guarantee life on this planet.

Biological diversity on the planet belongs to humanity. It should not be made into private property.

Respect for Cultures and Ethnic Identities

Throughout history, international trade has brought diverse peoples and cultures together. Rather than eliminating cultural and ethnic diversity, trade agreements should respect diversity and promote it. For example, multinational companies should not be permitted to push indigenous groups out of the jungle in order to harvest lumber.

The Principal Agreements of the International Labor Organization (ILO)

- **The Right to Organize Freely (**Agreement #87): Workers have the freedom to organize unions without suffering reprisals from management.

- **The Right to Unionize and Bargain Collectively** (Agreement #98): Collective bargaining is negotiating working conditions and remuneration between management and the union.

- **Equal Pay for Women and Men** (Agreement #100). Men and women should receive the same wages for similar jobs. Women should not be paid less just because they are women.

- **Maternity Protection** (Agreement #103)

- **Elimination of the Worst Forms of Child Labor** (Agreement # 182)

- **Prohibition of Forced Labor** (Agreements #29 and #105)

Respect for Human Rights

Human rights include economic, social, and labor rights. But currently, neoliberal globalization is promoting social dumping. Companies are lowering the costs of production by sacrificing workers' rights. They are reducing wages, eliminating ben-

efits, and busting unions. The alternative proposal demands that trade agreements not go against the interests of working people. Unions all over the world are also proposing that trade agreements include the basic norms for protecting labor rights already expressed in the International Labor Organization (ILO) agreements.

Respect for the Sovereignty of Nations

Trade agreements promoted by the World Trade Organization put transnational corporations above governments to the point where corporations can even sue governments if they get in the way of corporate profits. The alternative proposal reverses the direction of power and allows governments to control the transnationals.

Citizen Participation in Negotiating Trade Agreements

Trade agreements between countries and within the WTO are made secretly, behind people's backs. They don't take into account the thoughts and proposals of peoples' organizations and the rest of society. If governments inform the people at all about the content of the agreements, many times it's after the agreements have already been signed. Because of this, the alternative proposal is for grassroots groups and social justice organizations to be present during the negotiation of all trade agreements. When the agreements discussed are very important, the entire population should be consulted.

Cancellation of the Foreign Debt

The alternative movement has been very firm about proposing the cancelation of foreign debt. According to the Economic Commission for Latin America (ECLA), the foreign debt doubled between 1990 and 2000, going from $439 billion to $750 billion.

Many countries can't get out of poverty because they have to use the majority of their resources to pay the debts they owe to international financial organizations. They are condemned to pay eternally. The alternative proposal doesn't talk about "forgiving" the debt; it talks about debt cancellation because in reality the debt has already been paid many times in interest payments and in other ways.

Conclusion

All of these proposals favor designing fair and equitable international trade, so that trade between countries can contribute to a more healthy, interdependent world, where poverty and inequality do not exist.

Bibliography

Argumedo, Alcira, Pobreza y desigualdad en el Mercosur, *Buenos Aires Oculta.*
www.rebelion.org/economia/htm [August 25, 2001]

ATTAC, El ALCA en síntesis, *ATTAC Mendoza-Argentina*
www.rebelion.org-economia-htm [March 29, 2001]

ATTAC, ¿Qué es el ALCA?
www.rebelion.org-economia-htm [December 29, 2000]

Declaración de la II Cumbre de los Pueblos de las Américas
www.asc'hsa.org-declaración2.html [June 23, 2001]

García, Joaquín y Velázquen, Juan, Reflexiones sobre la OMC, *Cultura para la esperanza*
www.rebelion.org-economia-htm [August 23, 2000]

Ibisate, Javier, Génova de triste recuerdo, *Carta a las Iglesias 479 (2001) pp. 15-16.*

Ibisate, Javier, El Area de Libre Comercio de Las Américas: ¿Sueño o pesadilla? *Carta a las Iglesias 480 (2001) pp. 14-15.*

Khor, Martín, Porqué las formas de vida no deberían ser patentadas, *Revista del Sur 110,*
www.revistadelsur [May 15, 2001]

Menean, Georges, Cinco puntos esenciales relativos a las multinacionales, *ATTC*
www.rebellion.org/economia/htm [July 6, 2001]

Pérez, Ramírez, Pedro, La globalización de la resistencia contra el neoliberalismo, *Colectivo CRALED, Cuaderno de Materiales de Ensayo [May 15, 2001].*

WTO website, What is the WTO? *www/wto.org/indexsp.htm*

UNIFEM, El progreso de las mujeres en el mundo, 2000, *Informe Bienal de UNIFEM.*

Resources

For more information on fair trade, the anti-globalization movement, and alternatives to NAFTA and the FTAA, consult the following organizations:

Convergences of Movements of the Peoples of the Americas (COMPA)	www.compasite.org
Ecumenical Program on Central America and the Caribbean (EPICA)	www.epica.org
Fair Trade Resource Network	www.fairtraderesource.org
Focus on the Global South	www.focusweb.org
Hemispheric Social Alliance	www.asc-hsa.org
International Forum on Globalization	www.ifg.org
Jobs With Justice	http://jwj.org/global/global.htm
Kensington Welfare Rights Union	www.kwru.org
Public Citizen Global Trade Watch	www.publiccitizen.org/trade
United For a Fair Economy	www.unitedforafaireconomy.org
Web Community of Social Movements	www.movimientos.org
World Social Forum	www.forumsocialmundial.org

Also Available from EPICA

Economic Literacy Series in English

Ten Plagues of Globalization (EPICA, 2002)

In Spanish

Libre comercio. . . libertinaje de las trasnacionales
(original Spanish version of this book)

10 plagas de la globalización neoliberal

La privatización: o el nuevo colonialismo

El neoliberalismo

Con la sartén sin el mango:
El trabajo doméstico, base invisible de la economía

22 clavos y claves de la globalización

Globalización de la economía

This series is produced by the Salvadoran popular education team: Equipo MAIZ.
They each explain basic concepts of the world economic order in a way that everyone can understand.

Popular Education Techniques

Vamos a jugar, no. 1

Vamos a jugar otra vez, no. 2

Vamos a jugar de nuevo, no. 3

Full of step-by-step learning games, this series is perfect for anyone who teaches or leads group activities. Suitable for adult education as well as younger audiences.

EPICA • 1470 Irving St. NW • Washington, DC 20010 • 202/332-0292
epicabooks@epica.org • www.epica.org